WHAT IS ART?

Sculpture

KAREN HOSACK

www.raintreepublishers.co.uk
Visit our website to find out more information about Raintree books.

To order:
☎ Phone 44 (0) 1865 888112
📄 Send a fax to 44 (0) 1865 314091
💻 Visit the Raintree Bookshop at www.raintreepublishers.co.uk to browse our catalogue and order online

Raintree is an imprint of Capstone Global Library Limited, a company incorporated in England and Wales having its registered office at 7 Pilgrim Street, London, EC4V 6LB – Registered company number: 6695582

"Raintree" is a registered trademark of Pearson Education Limited, under licence to Capstone Global Library Limited

Editorial: Adam Miller, Charlotte Guillain, Clare Lewis and Catherine Veitch
Design: Victoria Bevan and AMR Design Ltd
Illustrations: David Woodroffe
Picture Research: Mica Brancic and Helen Reilly
Production: Victoria Fitzgerald

Originated by Dot Gradations Ltd, UK
Printed and bound by CTPS (China Translation & Printing Services Ltd)

ISBN 978 1 4062 0938 9 (hardback)
12 11 10 09 08
10 9 8 7 6 5 4 3 2 1

ISBN 978 1 4062 0945 7 (paperback)
13 12 11 10 09
10 9 8 7 6 5 4 3 2 1

British Library Cataloguing in Publication Data
Hosack, Karen
  Sculpture. - (What is art?)
  1. Sculpture - Juvenile literature 2. Sculpture - Appreciation - Juvenile literature
  I. Title
  730
A full catalogue record for this book is available from the British Library.

Acknowledgements
The publishers would like to thank the following for permission to reproduce photographs:
©AKG p. **19** (Robert O Dea); ©Andy Goldworthy p. **12**; ©The Bridgeman Art Library pp. **6** (Christie's Images), **17** ©The Bridgeman Art Library, **17** (© Succession Marcel Duchamp/ADAGP, Paris and DACS, London 2008), © DACS /Vera & Arturo Schwarz Collection of Dada and Surrealist Art), **22** (Private Collection), **27** (Private Collection, Photo © Christie's Images); ©Corbis pp. **4** (Gianni Dagli Orti), **5** (Francis G. Mayer), **14** (Jason Hawkes), **18** (Mike McQueen), **21** (Kieran Doherty/Reuters), **24** (Richard Cummins), **26** (Sandy Felsenthal/© Succession Picasso/DACS 2009); ©Gerard Scarfe p. **25**; ©Getty Images p. **20** (The Image Bank/IC Productions); ©Hawaiian State foundation of Culture and Arts/Satoru Abe East and West 1971 p. **11**; ©istockphoto p. **13** (Sami Suni); ©Martin Creed p. **16**; ©Rex Features p. **8** (Dazed & Confused); ©Copyright Estate of Robert Smithson, Courtesy James Cohan Gallery, New York p. **9**; Scala Archives p. **10** (© Calder Foundation, New York/ DACS London 2009/Museum of Modern Art); Scala pp. **15** (Photo Art Media/HIP/Scala, Florence), **23** (Digital image, The Museum of Modern Art, New York/Scala, Florence/© DACS 2009); ©Werner Foreman Archives p. **7**.

Cover photograph of Rodin's hand study in plaster. Plaster hands, a study moulded by Auguste Rodin, are displayed at the Musee Rodin in Paris reproduced with permission of Corbis/Bob Krist.

Every effort has been made to contact copyright holders of any material reproduced in this book.
Any omissions will be rectified in subsequent printings if notice is given to the publishers.

Disclaimer
All the Internet addresses (URLs) given in this book were valid at time of going to press. However, due to the dynamic nature of the Internet, some addresses may have changed, or sites may have changed or ceased to exist since publication. While the author and publishers regret any inconvenience this may cause readers, no responsibility for any such changes can be accepted by either the author or the publishers. It is recommended that adults supervise children on the Internet.

Contents

Any words appearing in the text in bold, **like this**, are explained in the glossary.

What is sculpture?

A sculpture is usually **three-dimensional**. Paintings and photographs are flat, but you can often move around a sculpture. You can see it from different sides and may also be able to touch it.

Children make three-dimensional models from an early age. It seems natural for people to make shapes out of materials they find around them, such as sand, mud, or clay. You might have made some yourself, perhaps from play dough or even with your food when you were younger!

Discobolos, after a bronze statue by Myron, c.450 BCE

This Roman copy of a Greek sculpture was made over 2,450 years ago. It shows a man throwing a discus, which was a very popular sport at the time.

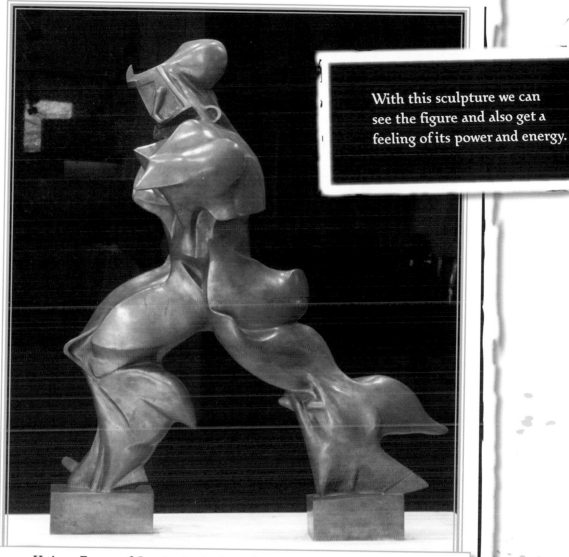

With this sculpture we can see the figure and also get a feeling of its power and energy.

Unique Forms of Continuity in Space by Umberto Boccioni, 1913

Both of these sculptures show movement. The sculpture of the discus thrower is carved from a hard material called **marble** and is more than 1.2 metres (4 feet) tall. The sculpture is very heavy and still, but the forward motion is clear and it looks as if the figure is almost real.

The other sculpture was made less than 100 years ago. The figure is walking and it looks as though it is pushing into the wind. The artist has included what he thinks the force of the wind might look like.

Looking at sculpture

You might think that you do not know much about sculpture, but if you ask a few questions about what you can see, you can enjoy looking at it. A good place to start is thinking about why someone might have made the sculpture. What do you think the artist was trying to tell us with the piece of sculpture below?

Look at this very famous sculpture. You can probably guess that the figure is thinking deeply about something. In fact this sculpture is called 'The Thinker'. What might the person be thinking about?

The Thinker by Auguste Rodin, 1880

This mask was used for special occassions. How do you think it would feel to wear it?

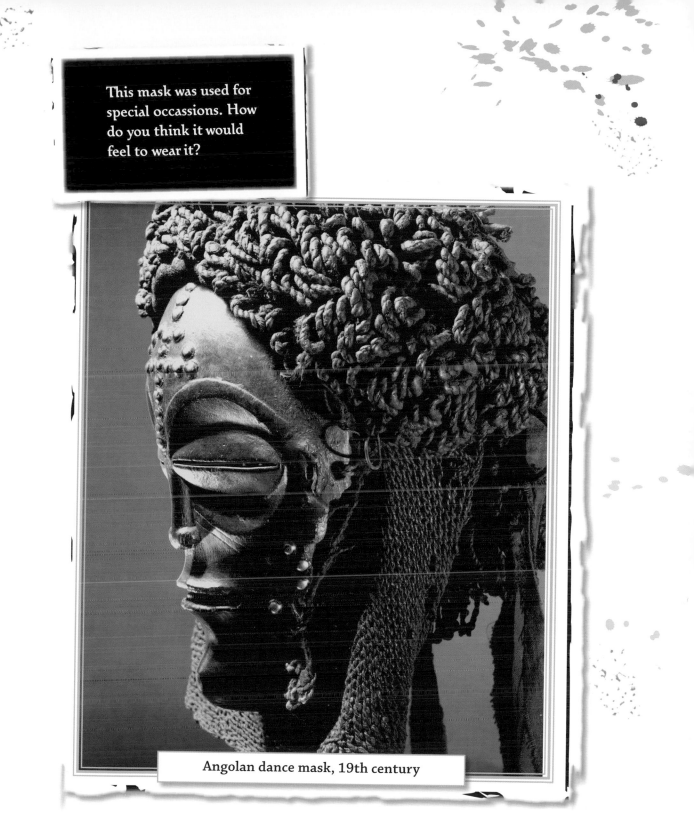

Angolan dance mask, 19th century

This beautifully-made mask was made to be worn in dance ceremonies. Masks are often used in rituals and for **spiritual** purposes. People all over the world often make sculptures to celebrate their beliefs. Can you think of any examples of this?

Finding clues

When you get to know some information about a sculpture it will help you to explore it more fully. Try to find out what the sculpture is made from. Then think about what this can tell you.

Self by Marc Quinn, 1991

This is a self-portrait of the artist. It is a **cast** of the artist's head made of nine pints of his own blood. The blood was frozen and kept refrigerated in a special display case.

Think about it!

Why do you think the artist used his own blood to make the sculpture? Warm blood flows around a living person, but here it is cold and still. Every person's blood has **genetic** information in it. Would it make a difference if the blood had come from another person, or even an animal?

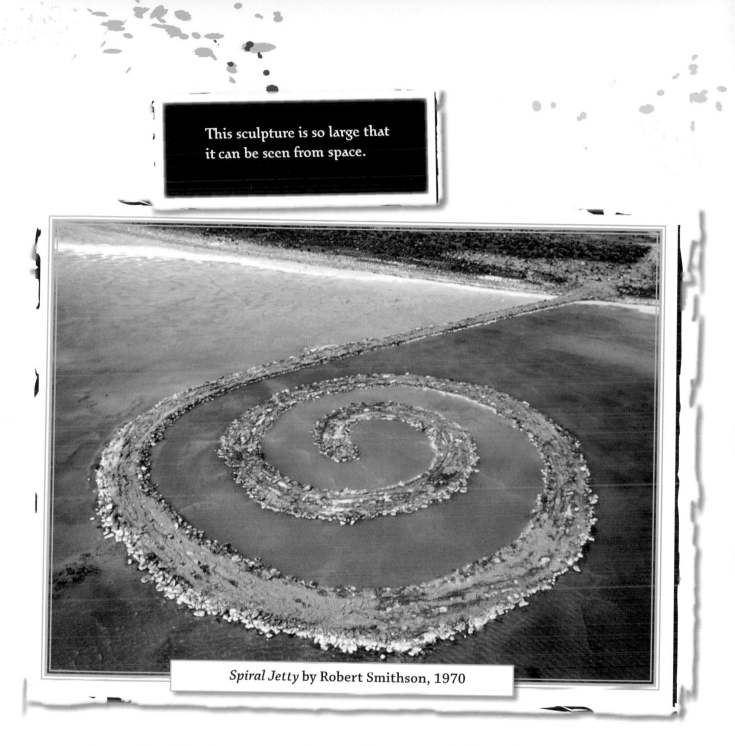

Spiral Jetty by Robert Smithson, 1970

In Utah, USA there is a sculpture that is made from huge rocks. The artist used 6,650 tonnes of rocks to construct the giant **spiral**, which is 460 metres (1,500 feet) long. The fact that it is made from natural objects in the open air and it is a natural spiral shape means that the sculpture looks as if it is growing out of the **environment**.

Natural inspiration

Many sculptors are inspired by nature. Look carefully at this mobile. Do the shapes remind you of anything? This time the title of the sculpture does not help you. Think about how the shapes might move in the wind. What words might you use to describe this? 'Floating' perhaps, or 'gliding'? There are no right or wrong answers. Art can mean different things to different people.

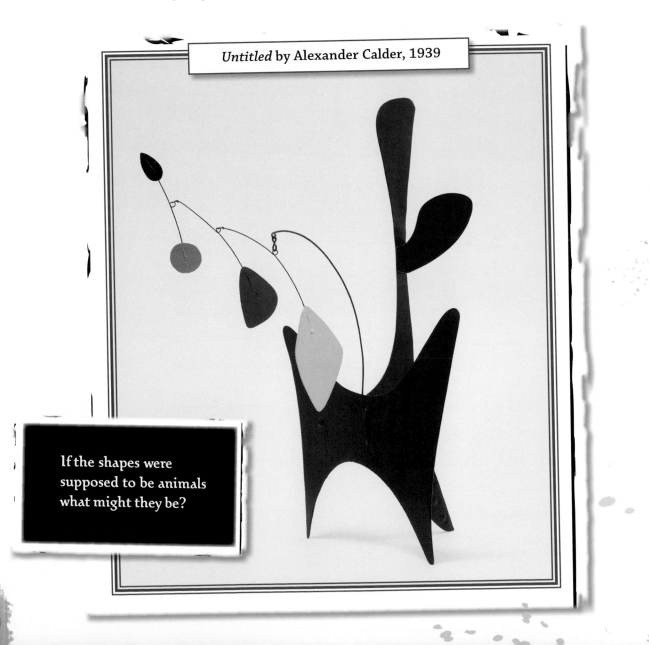

Untitled by Alexander Calder, 1939

If the shapes were supposed to be animals what might they be?

Why do you think this sculpture is called 'East and West'?

East and West by Satoru Abe, 1971

This sculpture is more clearly based on a particular natural form. The sculptor, Satoru Abe, is famous for using the **symbol** of a tree in his work. Think about what trees can stand for. They have roots that hold them in the ground. They have strong trunks which branch off and grow upwards towards the light. How would you describe this tree sculpture?

How long do sculptures last?

Sometimes artists decide to make sculptures from materials that they know will not last very long at all. This colourful piece is made from the leaves of a rowan tree. The artist has carefully sorted the leaves into their different colours and then placed them in position. He then took a photograph so we can see a record of the sculpture long after the wind and rain has made the sculpture disappear.

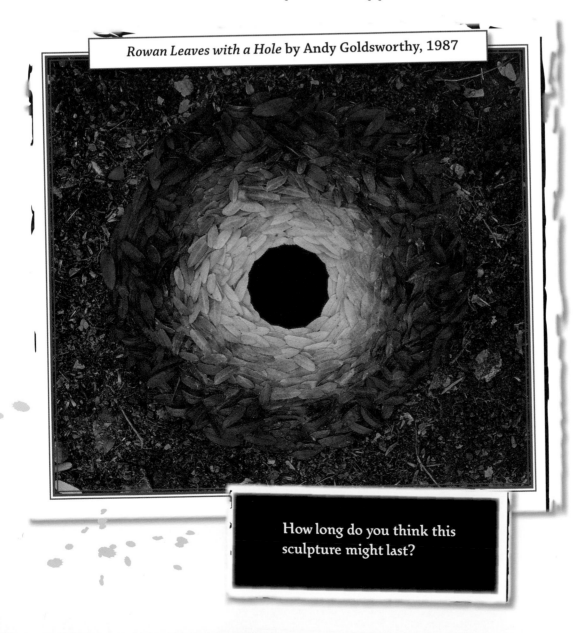

Rowan Leaves with a Hole by Andy Goldsworthy, 1987

How long do you think this sculpture might last?

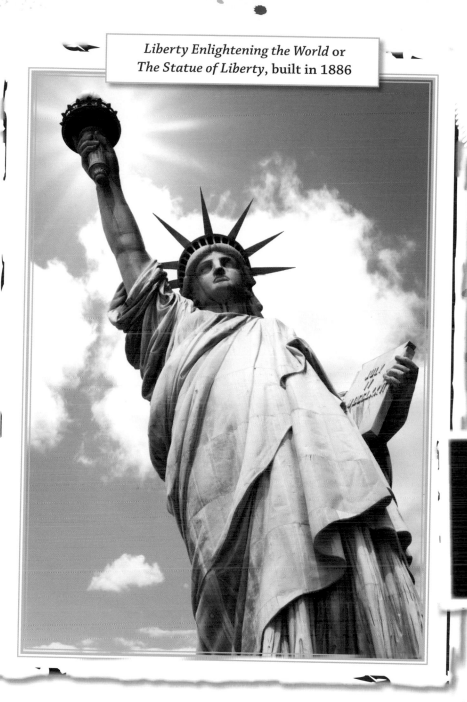

Liberty Enlightening the World or
The Statue of Liberty, built in 1886

Did you know?
People can visit a museum
in the base of the Statue of
Liberty. They can actually
see inside the sculpture,
through a special
glass ceiling.

The seven rays on the
crown represent the seven
continents, and the torch
is a shining light of hope.

This sculpture was designed to last a very long time. The French
and American people built the Statue of Liberty to celebrate the
American Declaration of Independence on 4 July 1776. It is
a **symbol** of freedom to millions of people all over the world and
an important work of **engineering**. It was made in 300 separate
pieces and the main body of the statue was shipped across the
Atlantic Ocean and put together in New York Harbor in July 1886.

Sculpture and symbolism

The Princess of Wales Memorial Fountain in London celebrates the life of a person. The water sculpture is a large oval ring made of granite. It is 210 metres (690 feet) long with grass in the centre where children can play. Water flows from two different directions and at different speeds, and this makes areas that bubble softly and others that are more rapid. The artist wanted to show how the princess's life was sometimes complicated and dramatic, and at other times it was calmer and peaceful.

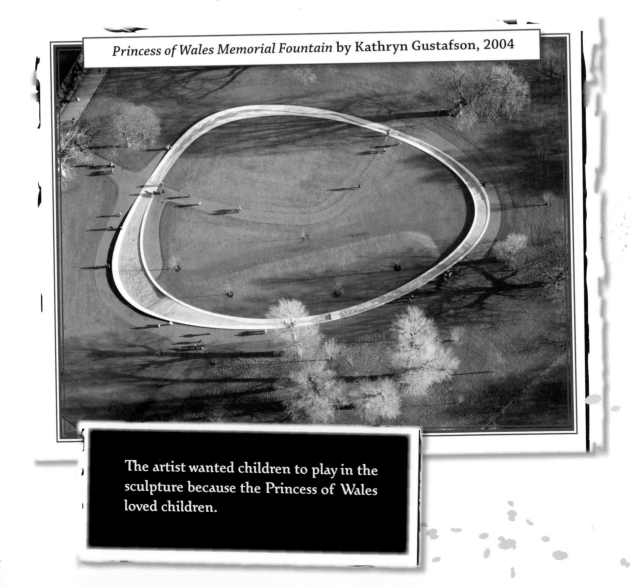

Princess of Wales Memorial Fountain by Kathryn Gustafson, 2004

The artist wanted children to play in the sculpture because the Princess of Wales loved children.

Art and war

World War I (1914–1918) was the first war to use mechanical weapons, such as machine guns and tanks. These machines were able to kill from great distances. Soldiers operating these weapons might not even know how many people they killed. Many artists, such as Jacob Epstein, tried to show the downsides to the age of machines.

Can you see what the figure is protecting inside?

The Rock Drill by Jacob Epstein, 1913–1914

The symbolism of this sculpture is very powerful. Look carefully and ask yourself what you are looking at. Can you make out a head or arms? It looks more like a cross between an animal and a machine than a human being. The sculpture makes us ask questions about what it is to be human at a difficult time. The artist made it at the time of political unrest in Europe before **World War I**.

Found objects

Is this a sculpture or just a ball of crumpled up paper? Can it possibly be both? Sculptures like this make us think about what art really is. Can art be made from any materials? The answer is yes. So, what turns this ball of paper into a work of art? Is it just because it is displayed as art? Could it be because the artist who made it called it art?

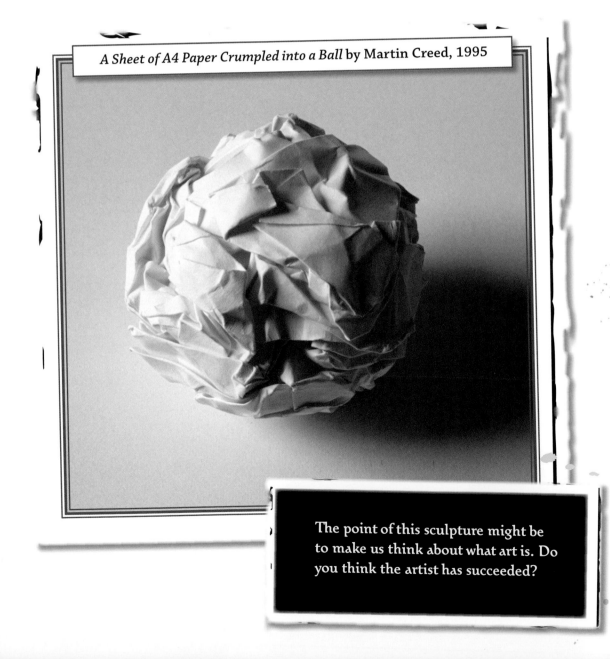

A Sheet of A4 Paper Crumpled into a Ball by Martin Creed, 1995

The point of this sculpture might be to make us think about what art is. Do you think the artist has succeeded?

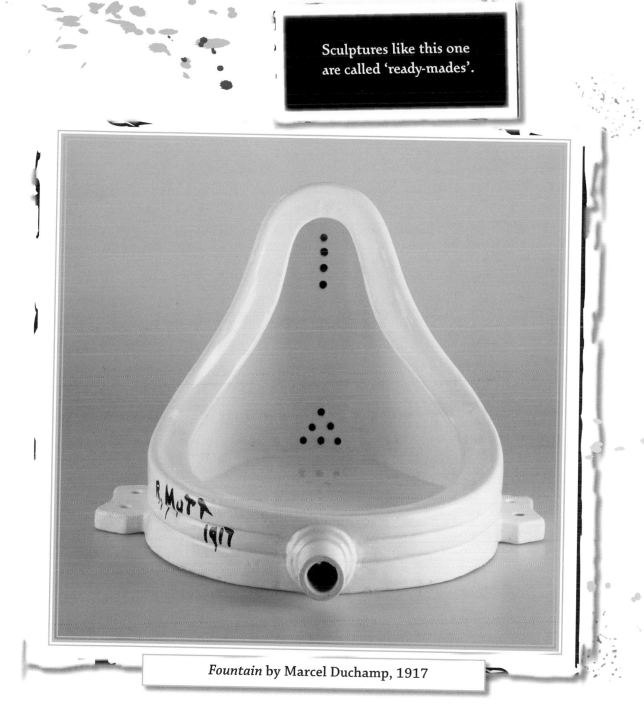

Fountain by Marcel Duchamp, 1917

Do you recognize this object? You are more likely to if you are
a boy! It is a urinal that is usually found in a men's public toilet.
The artist wanted to make people really think about what art is.
He wanted people to see that art did not always have to involve the
skill of making things well. He thought it could be about different
viewpoints. With this sculpture all he has done is taken an everyday
object and given it a title. He also signed it with a fake name.

Who was it made for?

When we know who a sculpture was made for it can help us to understand the meaning of the work. These figures were made for the Chinese Emperor Qin Shi in 210–209 BCE. They were buried with him to help him rule another empire in the **afterlife**. The public was never supposed to see them. In 1974, a farmer found the figures when he was drilling for water and they are now known as the Terracotta Army.

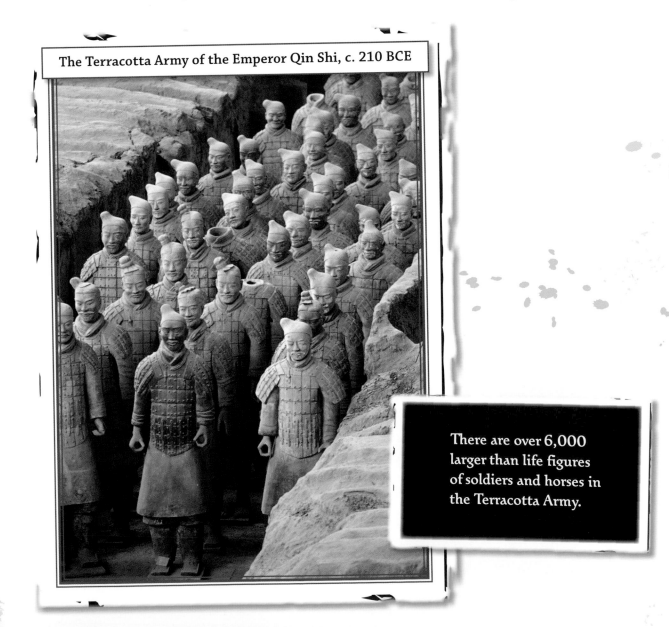

The Terracotta Army of the Emperor Qin Shi, c. 210 BCE

There are over 6,000 larger than life figures of soldiers and horses in the Terracotta Army.

The artist wanted this sculpture to be a **symbol** of love, warmth, and happiness. Or did he?

Puppy by Jeff Koons, 1997

This is a piece of sculpture that the public are definitely supposed to see. The 12-metre (40-foot) tall sculpture is made of steel, soil, and flowers. It has been shown outside various public buildings all over the world. Many people enjoy this huge, loveable sculpture with its cute name and beautiful flowers. The artist wanted to make people happy but could he also be poking fun at the world of art?

Huge sculptures

The public is supposed to get fully involved with both of these sculptures. *Cloud Gate* is a 110-ton stainless steel sculpture in Millennium Park, Chicago, USA. It has a 4-metre (12-foot) high arch under it, a bit like a gateway. People can wander underneath the sculpture and see reflections of themselves, the city skyline, and the clouds. The images they see are constantly changing.

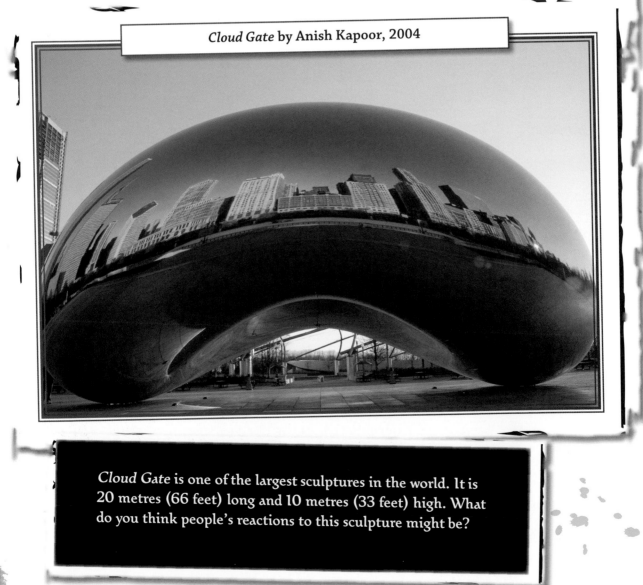

Cloud Gate by Anish Kapoor, 2004

Cloud Gate is one of the largest sculptures in the world. It is 20 metres (66 feet) long and 10 metres (33 feet) high. What do you think people's reactions to this sculpture might be?

Walking inside this sculpture is strange because you do not know which direction you are going. Why do you think the artist wanted this?

Blind Light by Antony Gormley, 2007

Blind Light is a sculpture that people can wander inside. It is a large glass box that can fit up to 25 people at one time. Inside, you can't see anyone else because there is thick **water vapour** filling the air. It can be hard to find your way out! People inside the sculpture look like part of the art from the outside.

Look again!

At first the meaning of a sculpture might not be clear, but it is always a good idea to look again.

> Abstract art can be difficult to understand at first. It is often open to lots of different interpretations. What does this sculpture say to you?

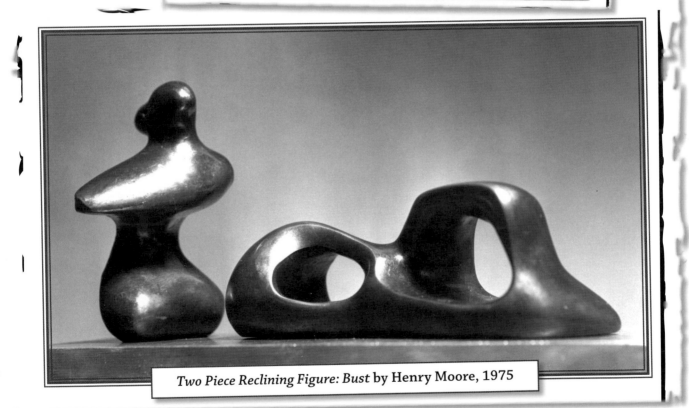

Two Piece Reclining Figure: Bust by Henry Moore, 1975

These two pieces look like smooth pebble-like shapes placed together. Could they be anything else? Could they represent, or stand for, something? If so, what might they represent? The artist Henry Moore simplified the shapes he saw in the human body. We call these sculptures **abstract** because they are taken from an original **source**, but have been changed into something else.

Surreal

Meret Oppenheim was considered a Surrealist. That meant that she tried to create works that were more dream-like than real. Surrealist art was never logical or easy to understand. Different people can look at a Surrealist work of art and come up with very different ideas of what it might mean.

Would you want to drink from this cup?

Object (Fur-covered Cup, Saucer and Spoon) by Meret Oppenheim, 1936

This is an everyday set of objects, including a cup, saucer, and spoon. The odd thing is that they seem to be made out of fur. The original source of this sculpture is very clear, but the artist has changed the meaning of the ordinary objects by using totally unsuitable materials. What is the point of a cup that cannot be used? Where else might you find such odd ideas? In dreams, perhaps?

The unexpected

Some sculptures look straightforward to begin with, but then have an unexpected twist. This sculpture is of a spoon and a cherry, which would be a very ordinary sight in a kitchen. But the sculpture is in a park and is also the size of a bus! What would you think if you stumbled on this sculpture when you were out for a walk?

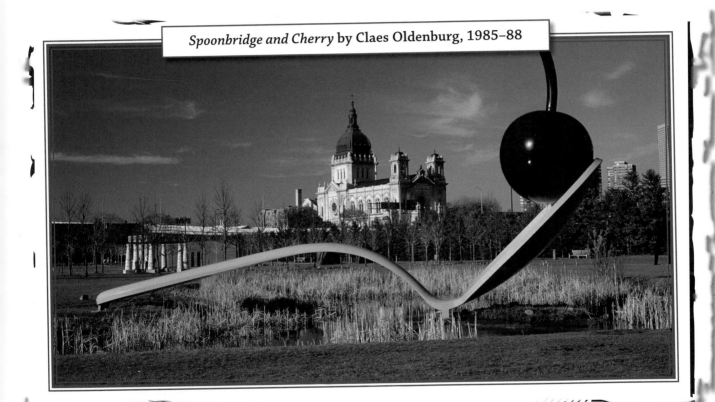

Spoonbridge and Cherry by Claes Oldenburg, 1985–88

Spoonbridge and Cherry is a fountain sculpture. It stretches across a small pond and a stream of water flows over the cherry.

Think about it!

The sculptor who created *Spoonbridge and Cherry* once said, "Very often I am sitting at dinner and I take out my notebook. I get very inspired when I eat, for some reason."

Chairman Mao by Gerald Scarfe, 1971

This is a light-hearted sculpture made by an artist who is famous for looking at world leaders in his work. Here he plays with the meaning of the word 'chairman'. A chairman is a person who leads a meeting or a group of people. The artist has used the word literally by actually shaping a chair into the image of a man. In this case the man is Chairman Mao, who was a leader of China in the 20th century.

Exploring sculpture

In this book we have looked at many different sculptures. Some have been small, others huge. Some have been made from traditional materials, such as **marble** and clay. Other sculptures have been made from found objects, and even the artist's own blood. We have thought about what artists might be trying to say in their work, but we have also thought about what the pieces might mean to us personally.

Art is very powerful and can encourage strong reactions from individuals. This can be clearly seen when a piece of public sculpture is put in a place where people often visit.

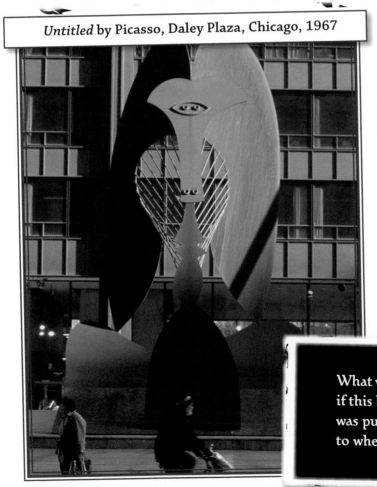

Untitled by Picasso, Daley Plaza, Chicago, 1967

What would you think if this large work of art was put in a place near to where you live?

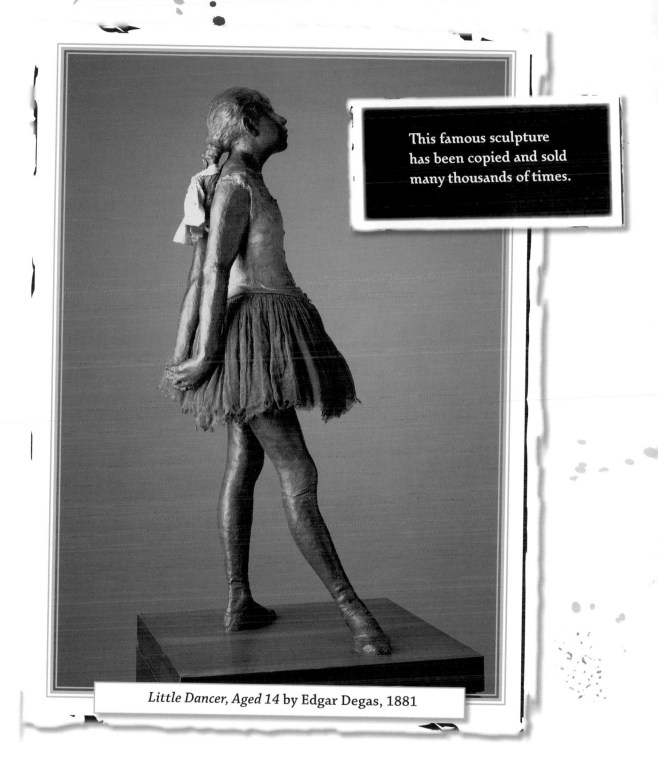

Little Dancer, Aged 14 by Edgar Degas, 1881

Less **abstract** sculptures can sometimes appeal to people more because they can easily recognize the subject. It is important to try and give all art some time and thought. You might discover something in an abstract sculpture that you did not see at first. You do not have to like everything, but with an open mind you might be pleasantly surprised and find something new and interesting!

Timeline

Where to see sculpture

This map shows where some of the sculptures in this book can be seen.

① Shaanxi Province, China
   The Terracotta Army

② London, UK
   British Museum:
      Discobolos, after
      Myron
   The Royal Academy:
      *Little Dancer Aged
      Fourteen*, Edgar Degas
   Tate Britain: examples of
      Moore's work
   Hyde Park, London:
      Princess of Wales
      Memorial Fountain

③ Paris, France
   Musee Rodin:
      The Thinker, Rodin

④ New York City, USA
   The Statue of Liberty
   Museum of Modern Art:
      The Rock Drill, Epstein
      Object (Fur-covered
      Cup, Saucer and
      Spoon), Oppenheim

⑤ Chicago, USA
   Chicago Daley Plaza:
      Untitled, Picasso

⑥ Hawaii, USA
   Hawaii State Art Museum:
      East and West, Abe

⑦ Minneapolis, USA
   Minneapolis Sculpture
   Garden:
      *Spoonbridge and
      Cherry*, Oldenburg

Glossary

abstract art not meant to look like real life, but which shows feelings or an idea

afterlife where some people believe they go after death

American Declaration of Independence an act in 1776 which formally separated the United States from British rule

cast something shaped in a mould

engineering the way things are designed and constructed

environment the natural and man-made surroundings, which plants, animals, and people live in

genetic information in molecules that make up animals and plants

marble limestone that is highly polished

source where something begins

spiral coiled shape

spiritual to do with the spirit, not physical or of this world

symbol something that represents something else

three-dimensional when an object has height, width, and depth

water vapour moisture from water suspended in the air

World War I 1914-1918 war between the Central Powers (Germany, Austria-Hungary and Turkey and Bulgaria) and the Allies (Britain, France, Russia, Italy, and the USA)

Learn more

Books to read

Shape (How Artists Use), Paul Flux (Heinemann Library, 2008)

Sculpture (Stories in Art), Rob Childs and Richard Spilsbury (Hodder Wayland, 2008)

What is a Sculpture? (Art's Alive), Anne Civardi (Franklin Watts, 2007)

Websites to visit

Get inspired at The Art Kids Site!
www.artkids.co.uk

View biographies of modern sculptors.
www.modernbritishsculptors.co.uk/sculptors

Visit the Tate Gallery kids website.
www.tate.org.uk/kids

Index